VESSEL

VES

SEL

Poems

PARNESHIA JONES

MILKWEED EDITIONS

Published 2015 by Milkweed Editions
Printed in Canada
Cover design by Mary Austin Speaker
Cover art by Mildred Howard
Author Portrait by Susan Aurinko
15 16 17 18 19 5 4 3 2 1
First Edition

Milkweed Editions, an independent nonprofit publisher, gratefully acknowledges
sustaining support from the Lindquist & Vennum Foundation; the McKnight
Foundation; the National Endowment for the Arts; the Target Foundation; and other
generous contributions from foundations, corporations, and individuals. Also, this
activity is made possible by the voters of Minnesota through a Minnesota State Arts
Board Operating Support grant, thanks to a legislative appropriation from the arts and
cultural heritage fund, and a grant from the Wells Fargo Foundation Minnesota. For a
full listing of Milkweed Editions supporters, please visit www.milkweed.org.

Library of Congress Cataloging-in-Publication Data

Jones, Parneshia.
[Poems. Selections]
Vessel / Parneshia Jones. -- First edition.
    pages cm
ISBN 978-1-57131-467-3 (alk. paper) -- ISBN 978-1-57131-914-2 (ebook)
I. Title.
PS3610.O62755V48 2015
811'.6--dc23
                                    2014038729

Milkweed Editions is committed to ecological stewardship. We strive to align our book
production practices with this principle, and to reduce the impact of our operations
in the environment. We are a member of the Green Press Initiative, a nonprofit
coalition of publishers, manufacturers, and authors working to protect the world's
endangered forests and conserve natural resources. Vessel was printed on acid-free 100%
postconsumer-waste paper by Friesens Corporation.

For Mary Ella Starling (1933-2011) and
Howard Antoinne Jones Jr. (1973-2008),
love doesn't even begin to cover it.

VESSEL

VESSEL

GIRL

Cocoa butter knees dancing
between two brotherly roads,
daydreaming, pretend out loud
Girl.

Singing off-key, flowing T-shirt hair,
microphone brush and missing front teeth.
Jackson 5, Culture Club, Whitney Houston,
Deniece Williams back up the deep-
voiced, juke joint, Midwestern-raised
Girl.

Catfish, crab legs, and chitlins
served on three-generation China.
Great Lakes, mason jars, fried pies,
and Mary Jane—wearing Girl.

Stained glass Sundays, training wheels,
wind, and a wide nose, thick plait, nappy back,
dimple in each cheek Girl.

Heiress of big legs, triple hip,
raised eyebrow, silver dollars,
dusty maps, and a diamond bracelet
Papa gave the day you graduated
eighth grade, and he said young lady
but hugged you like his little
Girl.

The only daughter
of an only daughter left;
the keeper of ash and memory,
curtsies and curiosity,
Easter poems, skinned knees,
polyester, silk, and calamity

Girl

stays close, superstitious,
sassy and studied.

Know better in your gathered years
of woman, grown, change-filled
coffee cans, kitten heels, cat calls,
and collateral, Girl is forever.

Let that Girl settle between new grays,
laugh-out-loud lines, and the sand
of her hourglass filling with fierce
each newborn day.

Girl stays forever.

I

What would happen if one woman told the truth about her life?
The world would split open.

MURIEL RUKEYSER

Definition

Parnassus [pɑːnæsəs]

n

1. a mountain in central Greece, just north of Delphi, that rises to a height of 8,064 feet (2,457 m). Held to be sacred by the ancient Greeks, it was associated with Apollo and the Muses and was regarded as a symbol of poetry. Greek name Parnassós.
2. (Literature / Poetry)
a. the world of poetry
b. a centre of poetic or other creative activity
3. (Literature / Poetry) a collection of verse or belles lettres

Parneshia [par: knee: she a]

n

1. 1980—daughter of high school sweethearts (prom queen and football captain). Father,
a Creole southern rolling stone, watches an old Greek movie, hears the word Parnassus. Father told it to Mother. Mother, first generation Northerner, couldn't understand what Father was saying (Greek doesn't roll easy off the Creole tongue). Mother shaped the word herself while baby moved about in her belly.
2. (Woman / Poet)
a. rooted in her Midwest, in her poetry
b. growing up in Mama's kitchen and stacks of dusty books
3. (Woman / Poet) twenty years later, the Poet searches the definition of her name...who knew

Naiad

A philosopher asked, If you could have one super power
what would it be?

When I was a little girl,
I spoke indigo—
birthed with gills passed
down from sea women.

I spoke indigo in my dreams.
My laughs and grandmother's
sweet water lullabies conjured waves.

I spoke indigo in my prayers,
praying for family and fins,
hoping my knobby brown knees
would morph into sienna scales
with fins of fuchsia.

I spoke indigo to my kin.
My grandmother's oceanic tongue
whispered in my seashell ears
our saltwater stories.

I wish for those little girl
sea lungs, pink as petals
blooming in rain.

I wish for the little girl
who dreamed in aquamarine,
the taste of a saltwater speech,
the nautical native tongue
speaking the language of the sea.

"Fair Trade"

During recess, Mary and I
carved our names into the dirt.

Mary,
such an easy, whimsical name.
Short.
I like short.

I watched Mary begin
with a mighty-shouldered M,
her angelic A, the R reaching
for the Y I always wanted.

MARY.
Short and sweet.
A name you never tire of writing.
I never had it that easy.

I could never find my name
on those miniature license plates.
No namesake characters on TV
or Bibled in verse. No Parneshia
had a little lamb.

PARNE...
Mary skipped around,
already finished with her four letters.
I was still on letter five of nine,

tired by *E*,
my arm aching the question,
why this name? Why so long?
Ask your mother, why such a riddle of a name?

PARNESHI...
Leaving off the final *A*,
I stared at Mary's crooked name
sprawled in the dirt.

Hey Mary, want to trade names?
Mines got so many letters!
Lots of great letters, Mary!

It's got a *P*, Mary, a *P*!
P, like princess. *A*, *R*,
Mary, *R*, like Roll-ups.
A, Mary, two of them,
like two angels in my name.

Mary, so sweet and easy,
shrugged her shoulders.
Okay, she said without hesitation.
You're Mary now and I'm PARNESHIA!
PARNESHIA!

My name is PAR-NE-SHIA!
I watched her twirl about
shouting my name, claiming it,
and a sense of panic came over me.

I want Parneshia,
my nine-letter riddle,
my *PARNESHI* and that last *A*,
the one I always wrote sloppy
because I never thought it
was as important as the first.

No! My name is PARNESHIA.
My Mama gave it to me!
It's mine and you can't have it, Mary!

Mary, hands on hips, skirt twisted,
chocolate milk stained to her top lip,
Okay. Let's go on the swings.
Mary, so sweet and easy;
so deserving of her short, sweet name.

PARNESHIA
I draw the last *A*,
make it count and stare
at my moniker: long, complicated,
hardly sweet, but mine.

LEGACY

for Evanston

We came with histories,
planted centennial stories along freshwater coasts.

An earthly heaven of emerald lagoons
and godly oaks shadow the chiseled
trails of our arrival.

We are the northern folktales.

Copper-back ancestors, with cotton-tipped,
woodcutter hands—
the heirlooms that built this landscape of jubilant
churches and miniature châteaus.

A harvest of migrating hearts
tell our way back when.
We are porch stories, buttermilk aprons,
lovers of Sundays and sailboats.

Land of dew-winged cardinals with chandelier
forests preserves our pioneers and preachers.

We are the long grass and anxious wind,
the generations, speaking softly, between
the lines of history.

DREAM CATCHER

for Mary Ella Starling

Rain falls softly with the slumbered
breaths of my grandmother.

I watch from the bedside,
trying not to disturb dreams of
watermelon patches and porch swings.

I walk slowly to the door.
The afternoon and freshly cut grass
cools down the room and eases
the drawl of summer.

Don't leave girl.

My grandmother lifts the quilt
sewn fifty years ago by her mother,
signaling me to join her.

I slide into the pocket of the quilt,
letting my grandmother's hands
cradle me back to child.
I nuzzle the crease of her neck
scented with grandfather's lips.

Her hands, more delicate than tears,
caress the roundness of my face.

Brings back memories, doesn't it girl.

As a child, my feet barely touched
her hips when she nestled me;
now our legs knit together,
creating a human quilt.
Sleep with good dreams girl.

Our eyes bow to the tranquil rain.
The deep breaths of our slumber
linger above us, like a prayer.

O.W. STARLING

for Papa

Crack the seal,
remove the cap,
and pour your life.

1932 Vintage, aged with

Fedora
Cigar
Rose
Red
Walker
Johnnie

Nothing to prove,
pour as slow as you want.

Long gone are days of hurry,
big band,
double shots,
back alley,
breakfast at midnight,
round the clock,
round the bar,
indigo,
shotgun,

shimmy,
shake down.

You about the quiet:
long walks,
easy does it,
win some, lose some,
close your eyes to remember.

Your old lady flirts from heaven.
Her purple dress, Elizabeth Taylor wig—
skin the color of buttercream;
you can taste her memory.

It's not that you still got it,
you just know how to keep it.
You know about that way back when,
that way, way back when
and that not too long ago.

Pour your slow song.
Sip the slow motion.

You
Rare
Reserve
Live to be savored.

For the Basement Parties at the YMCA

House of Pain and Pearl Jam
spill from oversized speakers.
Walls sweat, pooling the floor
with rhapsody and rhythm.
Pressed together, underground
surrounded by sound, thirteen
years of wondering comes down to
double dares and discoveries
in the black lights of the basement.

Boys drenched in their fathers' cologne
stand against cinder-blocked walls,
eyeing brand-new curves molded in
hip huggers.

Girls show imaginary cleavage,
with shy hips that haven't fully
mastered the switch.

Tie-dye scrunches and viscous gel slick
mounds of hair into onyx ice sculptures.

Bubonic berry Kool-Aid with hallucinating
quantities of sugar aphrodisiacs bodies
into bumping and grinding collisions.

Lenny Kravitz strings hips together,
sour apple Now & Later tongues
mix and match, hands disappear
in the dark under cut-off shirts
and baggy pants; exploring never
felt so good.

The bass rises past our knees, bodies float
in a wicked trance, clothes soaked with
Beastie Boys and lust.

We are the midnight hour.
Our acoustic heartbeats submerged,
not ready to come up for air.

BRA SHOPPING

Saturday afternoon, Marshall Field's, 2nd floor,
women's lingerie department

Sixteen: I am a jeans and T-shirt wearing tomboy
who could think of a few million more places to be
instead of in the department store, with my mother,
bra shopping.

Growing accustomed to these two new welts
lashed on to me by puberty, we enter into no-man's,
and I mean no-man-in-sight land of frilly lace, nightgowns,
grandma panties, and support everything.

Mama directs us to a wall covered with hundreds
of white bras, some with lace and little frills,
others with ribbons like party favors,
as if bras were a cause for celebration.

A few have these dainty, ditsy bows in the middle.
That's a nice accent don't you think? Mama would say.
Isn't that cute? Like this stupid miniature bow, in the middle,
will distract attention from my two looming, blooming issues.

When mama and I go brassiere shopping it never fails.
A short woman, with glasses attached to a chain around
her neck, who cares way too much about bras, appears.
May I help you, dearies?

The bra woman begins to assist my mother in finding me
the perfect bra to, as my mother puts it, *hold me in
the proper way. No bouncing please!*

Working as a team, they plot to ruin my entire day
with the bra-fitting marathon. They conspire handfuls
of white and mauve colored bras.
Who's making all these bras? I want to yell.

What size is she? The nosy bra woman asks.
You want something that will support them honey,
The bra woman winks while my mother inspects.
*Oh she's good size. She's way out of that training-bra phase.
I want her to have something that will hold them up proper.*

Them...them...them, she says.

Like they're two midgets I keep strapped to my chest.
I stand there while these two women, one my own kin,
discuss the maintenance and storage of my two dependents.

The worst is yet to come, the dressing room.
I hate the dressing room. Mirrors ready to laugh at me,
Women—half-naked—strapped, bulged, girdled into
    unbelievable,
torturous contraptions. Things showing that I hope to never
see on my own body.

I stand there half-naked and pissed.
Wasting away in a sea of bras—feeling like a rag doll

under interrogation with mama on one side,
the bra woman on the other, they begin fixing straps,
poking me, raising me up, snapping the back—
underwire digging my breasts a grave.

The bra clamps down, shaping my breasts into pristine
    bullets.
There is no movement, no pulse, no life, just still in their
uniformed perky salutes—real proper, like my mother
    wanted.

Why couldn't I have been born a boy?
I will never forgive my mother for this.
Blank face, my reflecting pout only produces lectures
from my mother about proper woman "upkeep."

After we are halfway through the bra inventory,
my mother takes mercy on me and gathers a select
few of hand-wash-only, neutral booby traps
and we make our way to the checkout counter.

I don't get happy too quick because I know
the bra woman continues to lurk, and if she
senses any excitement that this torture is over,
she will come with more white bras.

The bras are wrapped in pink papier mâché,
placed, by the bra lady, carefully into a shiny green

Marshall Field's bag. She hands it over to me as if
she is knighting me, and my mother oversees, satisfied.

We walk out of the underwire underworld.
Mom turns to me. *See, that wasn't so bad.*

II

If Thou be more than hate or atmosphere
Step forth in splendor, mortify our wolves.
Or we assume a sovereignty ourselves.

GWENDOLYN BROOKS
"God works in a mysterious way."

CONGREGATION

Weir, Mississippi, 1984

Sara Ross,
great- and grandmother of all
rooted things waits on the family porch.
We make our way back to her beginnings.

Six daughters gather space and time
in a small kitchen.
Recipes as old as the cauldron.
Aprons wrap around these daughters;
keepers of cast iron and collective.

Lard sizzles a sermon from the stove,
frying uncle's morning catch into gold-plated,
cornmeal catfish. Biscuits bigger than a grown
man's fist center the Chantilly-laced table
of yams, black-eyed peas over rice and
pineapple, pointing upside-down, cake.

The fields soaked with breeze and sun
move across my legs like Sara's hands.
Chartreuse-colored waters, the hide-and-seek
in watermelon patches, dim my ache for Chicago.

Peach and pear ornaments hang
from Sara's trees. Jelly jars tinted
with homemade whiskey,

guitar-stringing uncles who never left
the porch still dream of being famous
country singers.

Toothpick, tipped hats, and sunset
linger as four generations come from
four corners to eat, pray, fuss, and laugh
themselves into stories of a kinfolk,
at a country soiree, down in the delta.

FRENCH KISS

for Kenneth

Two weeks of boyfriend and girlfriend,
a holy matrimony of young.

The summer before high school
gives us lukewarm days at James Park,
trips to the gas station for blue Slurpees,
and ice cream sandwiches.

Barely cracking the code of thirteen,
we decide to honeymoon in the stairwell
of his parents' apartment.
Sweat and Dreamsicle-tinged fingers try
to find their place in all this confusion.

Should I put my hands here—like the movies?

Practices on pillows and back of my hand,
spying on my older brother's make out sessions,
sneaking in the double feature matinee
of *Indecent Proposal* and *Poetic Justice*,
determined to master Demi Moore's subtle
gaze at Robert Redford, or Janet Jackson artfully
sucking the lips off of Tupac—
me giggling with my girlfriends, boasting I could
do that with a boy named Kenny.

I talk too much.

Standing between our shadows, the window
lowers its sundial to give us afternoon mood lighting.
Our stomachs knot together, scared to keep
going—too scared to turn back now.

He tries hard to be the man in all this.
But there's no man here, nor is there woman—
just young, scared, and too late
to turn back now.

His eyes ping-pong back and forth across my face
as if I were a puzzle—a riddle he's trying to solve.

Don't be scared. Neither one of us can remember
who said it. He closes in on me, slow motion style,
just like the movies.

The tips of his fingers touch my brand-new hips
I, giraffe necked, lean back farther and farther
as he comes closer and closer, his lips an
"objects may appear larger than they are" situation.
This is not like the movies.

My eyes close and I try to see with my lips.
Waiting for the touch, we stop breathing.

Mouths position into a lock.
Weak knees almost make us lose our balance.

My top lip waits for his bottom lip,
my bottom lip quivering, chin and nose appalled,
trying to stay out of the way of the close encounters.

I hear our heartbeats, they jump-start my breathing.
Out of nowhere his lips move in a drawbridge motion.
My eyes pop open, stunned by the French connection.
I shut them back quickly as if I'm part of some tongue-
lashing horror flick. This is not like the movies.

Nice, he says, our faces flushed and flabbergasted.
I'm only capable of a cracked smile, too afraid of
what may come out or in.

Clammy hands interlocked, we return to childhood.

A playground of gawkers awaits, nosy girlfriends
wanting details, boys in high five position.
I'm whisked away for an emergency trip
to the gas station. My mouth still clenched
while inquiring girl minds want to know.

I burst into the Shell station doors, run straight
to the cooler reaching for the strongest Coca-Cola
I can find.

I chug my kiddie absinthe and tongue-tie
them with every twisted detail.
My girlfriends are amused and horrified.

We walk home. I'm still blushing and checking
that my tongue's intact, poking it out, asking my friends
if it looks different. *Would you do it again?*
I shrug my shoulders, knowing now
the power of talking too much and a slip
of the tongue.

Milk and Honey: Marvin Gaye

Father, father, everybody thinks we're wrong
Oh, but who are they to judge us
Simply because our hair is long
    —Marvin Gaye, "What's Going On"

How shall we write your story, Marvin?

Shall we begin with the tyrants and preachers
who shared the same body? The ones who told
you music was forbidden. How about your dreams
of being an aviator who could doo-wop?

Shall we go back to your sweet boy voice
lingering between needle and vinyl
of Etta James and Chuck Berry records?

Your three-octave croon
made women rethink their husbands
and *fine* rethink its definition.

Our struggles became your reckoning.
You rocked our heads and souls
back and forth in a cradle of lyrics,
asking the whole wide world,
What's going on?

Marvin, we can't forget your Tammi,
your sweet, sweet Tammi Terrell—

married only in song, gone too soon.
You never got over that, Marvin.
Neither did we.

I know, Marvin.
Some stories you wish to forget.
Some parts of you couldn't be saved
by your mama or the music.

The life you lived, between lines of darkness
turned you inside out.
Everyone knows the Devil, Marvin.
Even God.

Some will only remember you for your pain.
Some have your tears and speak your father's name.

The world hasn't changed much.
We still have wars and questions.

We try and hold on, play what's left of you.

Marvin, Marvin, how shall we tell
the story of you?

Press play.

Press repeat.

Make us want to holler.

Right on.

Two Lovers and a Pot
of Collard Greens

There's a simmer in my kitchen.
I crave collards, corn bread,
you.

Savory, slow-cooking, ancestor stalks
mist something southern and sacred.

Your kisses season my skin.
A delicious brew, slow-cooks
between the sheets as dusk
flavors the sky with darkness.

Collards steam with cayenne,
ham hocks, and whole Spanish onions,
dropped in a deep-sea pot.
Aromas speak a readiness—
curving a quiet language around the bed.

A ritual dish holds our tribal food,
scattered with black pepper,
and voluptuous tomatoes.

We feed each other collards and kisses
in bed while pot liquor absorbs
the last wet morsels of cornbread.

We surrender, sexual and satisfied.
Our fingers, licked slow, tuck themselves
between full bodies feasting on the night's heat.

Hearing Sylvia Plath's Voice, circa 1962

I am not very gentile. I feel that gentility is a stranglehold.

I expected something tragic.
A stumbled voice perhaps,
of hostage and brilliance,
shrouded in Waspy hesitation.

Your voice is siren, of sorts,
alive and aware, contradicting all your
posthumous—hiding dark between your breath.

The woman speaking seemed so sure,
so convinced she knew the exact value
of life and certain she could afford it.

Quick to answer, every response
dipped in adopted British Cockney
and the sureness of a Smith pedigree.
The metaphors of conversation were
an invite into a grand forest of a mind
where one could overlook the wilt and direness,
the suspicions of something off in the distance.

Peter Orr, in all his query, didn't know.
The poet's forest, with bottles hanging
from the trees, seemed harmless enough,
almost whimsical, like glass wind chimes

reflecting the sun, blinding the smoke screams
in the bottles.

The rifting of branches unplugs the vials.
The secrets, the pain released,
falling and imploding, puncturing tree trunks.

The screams behind the voice reveal her truth.
The truth too tragic, too late—only questions
and a garden of broken glass.

Haikus to Younger Self: A Suite

I

This is all you need
Passport, camera, rouge lips,
Money to get home

II

Fear is a feeling
Don't let it become a way
of life is too short

III

Sex is amazing
Try everything at least once
It builds character

IV

Your body—sacred
Love flaws and indifferent
They come in handy

V

Jones, kiss your brother
As if it will be the last
One day it will be

VI

Good food is so chic
Good wine, bourbon, martini
Well that's just swagger

VII

Learn to change a flat
Know how to drive a stick shift
The car and the man

VIII

Mom is always right
Only about stuff she knows
The rest—don't tell her

III

Living is no laughing matter.

NAZIM HIKMET,
On Living

Haiku for Bernice, Louisiana

My father born here,
Bernice, Louisiana.
Anyone seen him?

The Understudy

for Nate

Unbeknownst to us,
you knew all the lines.

You showed up, without rehearsal,
no direction given on how to make
two children from another father your own.
You came prepared to love what you didn't start.

You claimed your place in our lives,
grew yourself a branch on our tree—
You stuck around, stuck it out, and ended up
stealing the show.

You didn't have to take this part.
The downsides were plenty and messy
and still, you stayed.

It wasn't easy for either side.
Some days I wanted things to go back
to what they were: an inner circle of mother,
grandparents, and brother, before I knew the power
of what it meant to have a father,
even if it was just a figure, it mattered.
You made it matter.

I never stopped to think what it felt like for you,
having to memorize someone else's lines.
The lead never showed, but the show must go on.
And on it went, because of you.

Unbeknownst to us,
you knew all the lines.

Bravo, encore, take a long, deep bow.
Unbeknownst to us,
you were always the star.

BLINK

Love for a person, must extend to the crows on their roof.
—Chinese Proverb

Cooking dinner for one,

she prays over the steam,
stirring a pot of luck gone bad
black-eyed peas, rice religiously
simmering.

When she sleeps, pieces of memory
disappear, disoriented slumber.
I never thought she would lose
her memory, her need to remember.

She wakes up beautiful but scared,
forgetting names and misplacing thoughts.
Uncontrollable tempers and public tantrums,
I beg her to think back to yesterday,
back two seconds ago. She turns away from me.
I am a stranger.

She no longer desires her husband;
can't remember the first time she made love,
refuses to remember the last.
Grandfather walks away, leaving a trail
of fifty tears.

Her companions are nightmares and church.
She can always be found in the pew,
standing hollow in a freshly pressed
usher uniform, scented with Woolite,
lavender, and bay rum. Church is what
she lives for now. The only place she
remembers to go.

Great-grandma Sara used to say,
Some of the biggest devils go to church.
I wonder, has the church taken
my grandmother hostage?

Has the Baptist Sunday séance
smothered my grandmother
like a muzzle, keeping her from yelling
for help, yelling her awful truth, screaming
for her sanity?

She walks through the house, portraits of
ancestors bow their heads in shame
for the grandmother who should have carried
their stories, held them close, and kissed them
before passing them on.

I no longer hold my grandmother's hand.
I am a stranger.
I walk behind her now, hoping to catch
the last of what fades from her memory.

I still want to believe she is in there.
I want to take the last of her,
plant her in my heart and let her
bloom again, happy, saved.

Bitter Smell of Ashes

I stand by the silver bullet casket
waiting for you to come back to life.

Great-uncle.
Belly full of heavy laughs,
pockets holding shiny copper
and earth nickel coins.

A small gathering sanctifies you.
Your wife does not weep;
only one daughter of your three
mourns you enough to offer her tears.

Your men-children sit still and disturbed.
They echo your features but will never
tell stories of you to their children.

I knew the one they all wanted,
the sweet and tender father
they wished for; you were a sacred
carving in my kinfolk collection.

They knew someone else.
Your wife knew the tyrant
striking your life lines across her face—
fingers roped around her throat,
the noose of your marriage
loosens, setting her free.

She offers nothing in your death,
the badge of a broken wife
who stopped loving you long before
your last breath.

Your children pass your casket one by one.
No love or forgiveness, just a body left
hollow and haunted.

Your widow cinders you to ash,
lets you blow in the violent wind,
leaving no trace you ever existed.

GEORGIA ON MY MIND

for the children of Atlanta, 1979–1982

Children become ancestors
in the Georgia night.

Remember us.

Mamas and daddies
up all hours
pacing
searching for their murdered
angels with mutilated wings.

Kiss our mothers for us.

Some were never found,
soft bones swept under moss trees.
The missing and ache sweat
across the foreheads of fathers
reckoning nightmares.

Mothers scream in their pillows,
not wanting to close their eyes
to see the dead faces of their children.

Tell our fathers we love them.

We still search for them,

still believe they will come back to us
smelling of burnt peaches and baby's breath,
fresh and dewy-eyed, unharmed and happy,
we still pray they will come to us
in the night.

Remember us.

And we do,
lost children of Atlanta.
We remember the sounds of your vanishing,
the sounds of your fathers' hearts on fire,
and your mothers' wombs bursting.

House of Cards

There have already been 1.7 million foreclosure proceedings in the US in the first eight months of 2007, and up to 2 million families are expected to lose their homes over the next two years, according to estimates by the US Congress's Joint Economic Committee.

—from a 2007 BBC report

Rows of unfinished dreams,
half-acre plots of empty dwellings,
turn neighborhoods into ghost towns.

Sights of yellow and red stickers,
the modern day scarlet mark,
on new thermal-pane windows,
tells passerby its all too familiar fate.

Brand-new walls with incomplete copper
piping meant to filter water
into porcelain tubs to bathe splashing,
giggling babies and their rubber ducks.

The finest pine, bamboo, and oak
cut with precise corners, glazed in several
coats of polyurethane, make the hallways
look like paved strips of sweet brittle.

These floorboards will never squeak, settle,
or tell stories.

They will never kiss the bottom of bare feet,
pacing back and forth to rock those same
babies to sleep or wait up for love ones.

The ones who make themselves at home
are spiders, stitching their cobwebs
to exquisite crown molding.

There are other walls that have been lived in.
Lived in and memorized by old women
who paid for their homes with their hard-
earned lives and the hard-earned lives
of their dead husbands.

Their repossessed memories and foreclosed
hopes leave a stench no amount of ammonia
can suffocate.

Doorknobs corrode around the edges
with dried-up keyholes that forget they
are married to a key.

Dust tarnishes antique white walls,
fireplaces hum, stainless steel rusts,
closets become caves, yards become graveyards
of dead tea roses and lonely swing sets

and the porch light that has stayed on long
after everything has disappeared inside,
flickers a single family slide show, a fading
panoramic landscape of an American dream,
deferred.

Legend of the Buffalo Poets

for Frank X. Walker and the Affrilachian Poets

There is a rumble in his roaming.
Part bison, part thunder,
he is a stampede of words,
raising mountains from rooted earth.

He leaves a scented trail of bourbon
and misty coal-tipped pencils,
blackening the earth with his footprints.

The Native Americans hold him
sacred in their stories:
Black Katonka they call him.
He roams the Kentucky valleys.

Few have spotted him in the coal-black
mountains. Sometimes he grazes alone
and other times he travels with
a mystical tribe of Affrilachians.

Anyone that walks these bluegrass lands
knows the stories.
They know when thunder shakes the hills,
Affrilachians are writing.

When the sky mists over black,
Affrilachians are speaking with ancestors.

When the earth is warm and the
soil soaked with poetry,
Affrilachians have left their mark,
a trail buffaloed black.

Litany: Chicago Summers

Chicago has a strange metaphysical elegance of death about it.
—Claes Oldenburg

We are rapture, tundra,
the silk between concrete.

We are hallways of crying babies,
simmering neck-bones, sirens
across the ceiling's midnight.

Shirtless boys run into oblivion.
Their mothers' overtime eyes
never call in sick.

Caged ice cream trucks, El tracks,
the constant replay of Curtis Mayfield
offer a taste of a poor man's heaven...and hell.

We play in our shadows.
We are the televised, Technicolor,
inside-out dreams.
We are the preacher's sermons,
splintered pews, haunted graves
still looking for their rest in peace.

To love us, you must come armed
with an iron soul.

Love the broken wings, spoiled air,
the swollen hearts that have forgotten
how to dream. Love our delirious souls
running wild in this concrete jungle.

Love us enough to save us from ourselves.

Imagine our resurrection.

Our silk-screen babies baptized
in these Third Coast holy springs.
Imagine the Lake Michigan waters
washing jubilee into our streets.

Watch us closely.

Resurrection.

Be our witness.

IV

You only live once, but if you do it right, once is enough.

MAE WEST

STILL MEMORY

Photograph: Starkville, Mississippi, 1940

Six chocolate truffle girls line up,
holding hands.

Two with wide mouths missing baby teeth,
three with ponytails, two with afros,
all dressed in homemade skirts and coveralls.
Their bare butterscotch feet
gray in the picture but still sweet.

The shanty shotgun house
stills a history in the background.
Indigo bushes and ironwood trees
surround the antique porch.

These sisters will unlatch little hands,
grow into women and scatter
new lives across maps and borders.

One in Kosciusko,
one in Milwaukee,
two in St. Louis
living in a dead husband's house,
one in Joliet, stroked
to her death bed,

and the one holding the photo
sits in her Chicago apartment
holding all that is left of this memory
she can no longer recognize,
sisters she can no longer identify.

HABIT: SALT

For Harold's Chicken Shack and the would-be preacher

He could've been a preacher in another life.
Carrying a Bible and a kind word.
Instead, he carries a bottle of hot sauce
wherever he goes.

He's a regular in Harold's Chicken Shack.
The lady behind the counter knows him.
His eyes bulge out from too much
of the edible white nicotine.

I ain't supposed to eat salt, ya know
he says between asking the girl
behind the counter if she ever heard
the good sermons by the good Rev. Meeks.

Doctor said salt digging me an early grave.

So what you doing here then? The girl asks.

Well, I promise, after these six wings,
I'ma stop. Just one more time and I'm through.
You hear me back there?
The cook looks up to be his witness.

Now don't mix no fries wit my wings
cause I ain't supposed to have salt.

The girl rolls her eyes.
She hands him the over-the-counter drug,
wrapped in a golden batter with ribbons
of mild sauce that make it the most delicious,
artery-clogging present.

He turns to me.
It's bad for ya baby. I ain't nobody.
I'm just trying to give a little advice.
Salt ain't good for ya baby."

I am amused, confused, and concerned
for this man.

He salivates over the chicken
with both palms up to take his hit.
Chicken to lips, I swear he kisses it first
before biting down into grease and meat
that's had the Holy Ghost fried out of it.

His eyes close like an addict's;
feet can't stop moving, body shaking,
he begins to hum a spiritual like he's
been touched, like he's seen the light.

I look over at the girl behind the counter
popping her gum, shaking her head, and
checking her cell phone all at the same time.

She goes back to filling the jars of jalapenos
while Herb Kent reminds us it's Sunday
with dusties, the Chicago sidewalk-South Side-
anthems, smoking their way out of the speakers.

Yellow, caramel, and red velvet cakes
are showcased like rare edible jewels
at the front counter.

A black President's picture hangs crooked
on the wall, the tip jar empty, and the cook
is making fried chicken a religion.

Damn, so good, the man smacks softly.
He pulls out his hot sauce, gives it three shakes,
sits it down on the table, takes the top off,
lets it breathe like it's rare vintage
from the finest vineyard.

He pours the liquid lust over chicken
already covered in mild sauce,
lets a little get on his trembling hand
just so he has an excuse to lick
the chicken grease off his fingers.

He forgets his manners, mama's pops
to get elbows off the table, no napkin
in the lap, and grease glosses his lips.

Number 152, the girl calls out.
I take my chicken and head toward the door.
I look over at the man who could've been
a preacher carrying a Bible and a kind word,
who says that he ain't nobody.

But maybe he is somebody.
Someone who shouldn't eat salt;
a prophet carrying a bottle of hot sauce.

Chicago-Style Italian Beef

Do you want it dry, wet, or dipped...sweet or hot?

Take a trip to Planet South Side.
Stockyards of old world *ciao* and *arrivederci*,
turn-of-the-century Italians
unpack rolling pins and meat sauce
and the family secret—*sotto aceti*;
made under the Pope's Sunday blessings
and stone wall kitchens of rosaries and wooden spoons.

That secret sotto aceti, carried in glass jars,
in silk-lined suitcases across the ocean,
settled into garlic-scented kitchenettes,
nestled in neighborhoods hidden
in the south and west crevasses
of a big-shouldered city.

Big-hipped beef
spiced with Mama Francesca's pepper flakes,
or Mama Louisa's garlic mix, slow roasting,
don't rush it, you have time,
go make love,
carry out a vendetta,
pour the spumante,
write to the ones still walking the Colosseum streets
and tell them of this young country,
only a few hundred years old,

this midwestern place of wind, wide lake, and white lighting.
Tell them this is home now.

Razor the beef into whispers,
cascading into a baptism of its own broth.
Get the Italian roll drunk in au jus, pile it with beef
until the wet seams start to give way.

Now the sotto aceti, ahh the sotto aceti,
we will nickname it giardiniera—
this opera of peppers and pimento,
carrots, cauliflower, celery, and olives,
all bathing in oils and vinegars.
Let it drizzle over, down,
in-between the beef, slow down,
don't rush,
go make love some more,
drink more wine,
sit on your newly adopted stoop,
watch Chicago play its bluesy life,
miss the cobble streets of Rome,
let the giardiniera oil run down your arm,

This is home now. You made it so.
Eat and be close to God.

INSTINCT

Your fingers become long brown architects.
My blue-lined curves tangle with jubilation.
We recite our prayer books of precious places.

Flares lit, turquoise tongues rupture the mausoleum
between hips.

Upheavals of thighs, wrists, and waist—
pieces of me scatter with figs, macaroons,
emeralds, and ornaments—this treasure trove
we bury beneath a thickening of copper air.

Gripping the edges of the sheets, you
parachute over me as twilight bursts,
sprinkling a nutmeg dawn over our settling.

The half-eaten sun watches,
we hammock into a calm sway, sheets receding,
the ceiling fan humming—cooling down
the sleeping volcanoes.

ODE TO BOURBON:
A WRITER'S DISTILLERY

for the Spalding MFA tribe

The brethren of shape-shifters
summon me across two state
lines of flat, fertile distance.

Carolina coral, cast iron
tobacca tongues of Tennessee,
and tipped hats of seven boarders
distill bluegrass meadows.

Begin with nine years of cooling Creek,
a slow waltz on the Ohio,
and a symphony of cicadas.

Nights of bustle and Blantons,
secrets and steaks covered in béarnaise,
dripping on poems revealing themselves
from behind the red velvet curtains.

The seamstresses of stories dip
their hems in the musings of Woodford,
while tailors of tales wet their felt-tipped
pens in the legend of Pappy.

I try on all of my woman
and write myself a truth.

The shadow boxers of diction
pour their rusty champagne
down my translucent throat.

The poems write themselves
when the Dirty Bird gets loose
in the southern wild.

By morning we are history.
Angels and demons spooning themselves
in the charred oak barrels of journals.

The flask whistles a metaphor.
I'm still in my dancing shoes,
pen and pulse writing circles around me,
distilling a third eye and aged soul.

Torching the Stage:
Mitchell L. H. Douglas
and Donny Hathaway Meet

for Mitch, kicks and all

The poet sits at the bar
with his back to the stage.
His pages and lips, rimmed
at the edges with Knob Creek,
the country man's kerosene.

The musician emerges from dyes
of red and seamless purple lights
coming from the ceiling.

He adjusts a seat next to the poet,
signals for the same drink while
tugging at the hat he wears every day
of the week and only takes off when
entering church or his mama's house.

Are you ready? The musician asks.
The poet never takes his eyes
off his bourbon.
A black Man is always ready.

They release themselves from
the hips of the bar and move
like night to the stage.

The poet's words strike the mic,
flammable notes of soul release
from piano keys melting to the
musician's touch.

Music and poetry choke oxygen
out of the air. The poet inhales so deep
his rib cage soaks through his shirt
and he releases a metaphoric combustion
that engulfs the stage in flames.
The poet and musician trade only
one look before they disappear
into the inferno.

The lights change moods,
casting an illumination of blue vapors
that extinguish the blaze.

All that is left is the scent of cooked bourbon,
molten piano keys, splinters of stage,
and a cindered mic echoing ash.

TENDER

for Illy

She is curled half-moon
to the edges of the bed.
A new-mother sweat hinges
her temples contracting with delirious
motions of the son tracing her inside.

The humming of a swollen belly
releases ripples of warm ache
down into thighs, as her hips
break open her history.

He is a new chapter.
She lets him make peace
with first breaths of dry air;

In the haze of new,
they find huddled space,
pulse syncing their heartbeats,
in a re-mastered gestation.

V

I imagine one of the reasons people cling to their hates so stubbornly is because they sense, once hate is gone, they will be forced to deal with pain.

JAMES A. BALDWIN

AUTO-CORRECTING HISTORY

for President Barack Obama

Spell check does not recognize
this name—yet.

It tries, with a red underline alert,
to tell me that this is wrong,
that my letters are misplaced,
leading my complicated PC,
with its perfect vocabulary,
to believe no such name exists.

It offers suggestions to fix
what history has already confirmed.

These letters, roundabout, with all
their beautiful curves and angles,
their intricate folds forming perfect Bs
and As and the roundest O,
shaping a name that has awakened us all.

Barack and *Obama* cause keystroke duels
between my auto-correct and me.
Not willing to give up,
it plugs in *Brick* and *Abeam*, trying to
hold on tight to its King's English.

This name isn't a mistake.
No slip of the keys on my part.
No half-asleep or dazed typing,
no hurried rush of tidal wave words and wonder.

Every letter in this name comes with purpose.
Each keystroke is meant.
I highlight the name, click "add to dictionary."
I auto-correct my spell check.

It must be understood that he exists,
that we exist.

We are real and breathing.
We are hungry and rewriting dictionaries.
We are poets and presidents.
We have made it known that his name,
our names, every black letter birthed
from the blinking cursor is permanent
and correct.

SHUTTER

for Kelly, Ellen and David—Conjured to the bone

We are the two-headed city
the living covering the dead
the dead hovering the living

Kelly Norman Ellis, "PONTCHARTRAIN"

Still is the gift he gives.

Behind the shutter, in the crescent of a city,
three women become the voodoo,
in the aperture of a conjure man's eye.

They unpack their lives,
let loose their hips and copper manes.
The shape-shifting shutter of his lens
captures the supernatural, framing the metallic
silhouettes of beguiling superstition.

Daughters of dust and duende
feast on oysters in gravy, blue crabs and grits.
They leave a trail of tipped hats, low-country men
and gypsies who read the fortunes of the world
off their switching legs of revival.

Conjure Man watches this religion of women.
The streets of Rampart and Bourbon
become the dark rooms of the dancing dead.
The shutter retells the history.
Ghosts revealed in the flash.

Deities dance a boogaloo in the bayou.
The chants of Oya baptize the left-over,
still forgiving being left behind.
The women of dust and duende
release their voodoo.
Conjure Man shutters the black of this magic.
His looking glass salvages the saved.
Stills the born-again.

Resurrection under the Moon

But it be a gift, a gift
Out of they misery
I become blacker than the skin
of a tree in the rain,
and I be rooted
in the rich black earth.
Out of me flies the swallow.

Delores Kendrick,
The Women of Plums

I wait in the sugarcane fields.
We meet under the moon's watch.
He look tired and worn
like a walking corpse.

He hurtin' bad.
Master made sure he made his point
with slashed welts traveling like serpents
across his back.

He walk up to me cautious-like,
stare me right in the eyes
and somethin' in him come back to life.

He touch my hips,
like he can't believe they real.

My dress, I sews myself, he take a part,
real careful with each string and stitch,
like it be some fine tapestry.

He whisper my name a thousand times,
fearin' he might never speak it again.
You can tell how much a man love you
by the way he say your name.

He holds my name tight with his voice,
tracin' every syllable with his tongue,
lettin' it linger on his lips
like watermelon wine.

All the while he be memorizing my eyes,
afraid he gon' forget the color.

My smell, my potion of rose water
and lily, mixed with sweat and steam
from the hot water cornbread,
bring him back to the living world.

I tells him to lean on me,
his back crippled,
legs wilting like old oak branches.

His scent, coiled tight to his head,
and 'round the plains of his shoulders,
reach for me.
I smell the young in him,

hidin' from master and that whip,
kept quiet in the pockets of his neck.

We link together, so close
our skin begins to melt.
His kisses move about my face
like magnolia petals.

Their ain't no room for fear
when we lovin' each other,
this ain't for the takin', rapin',
or slavin'.
Master can't have this part of us.

I let him love me all night.
I know my lovin' keep him
from the slave grave.

black woman's love
ain't nothin' casual.
Our love brings our men
back from the dead.

DIVA SUITE

BLACK VENUS: JOSEPHINE BAKER

*I improvised, crazed by the music...Even my teeth and
eyes burned with fever. Each time I leaped I seemed
to touch the sky and when I regained earth it seemed
to be mine alone.*

— Josephine Baker

Get 'em Girl

St. Louie

Switch back

Street corner

Small-minded

Segregated

Simpleton

Slave driver

Think you slick

Saint Louie

Is you saint?

Is you sinner?

So long

See you later

New York

Renaissance
Renegade
Black and gold
Chorus girl
Shimmy shimmy
Charleston Chew
Beyoncé who?
Get 'em girl
Zoot Zoot
Ooo wee
Make 'em sweat
There she go
Cross the water
Round the world
Get 'em girl

Bonjour

City of Light
Tam tam
Tale unfold
Pomade
Belly button
Grass skirt
Banana split
Black pearl
Boogaloo
Caravan
Secret spy
Champs-Élysées

Get 'em girl
Sho' you right

Civil Rights
The only right
Take charge
Crusade
Controversial
Letting lose
Chateau
Carnegie
Get 'em girl
Keep the fight
Take the night

You got 'em now
Cosmo
Rainbow Tribe
Monte Carlo
Princess Grace
Peace and pride
Shimmer on
Shake 'em right
Sho' you right
Josephine
Tamberine
Titillate
Get 'em girl
Show them legs

You got 'em now
Don't stop
Keepin' classy
Count down
Champagne
Showstopper
Round the moon

Josephine, get 'em girl

NANNARELLA: ANNA MAGNANI

I'm deeply human and, even if you can't see it,
I feel I have much poetry inside. I'm very loyal...
very. It's enough, isn't it? Should be enough.

　　　　　—Anna Magnani

She appeared on the screen,
absolute and Roman.
Face chiseled from mausoleum stone
crowned by an explosion of obsidian hair—
eyes cratered in shadows of truth and tragedy.

In the land of Duse,
before Meryl and Sophia,
There was Magnani. Nannarella—
the perennial toast of Rome.

She erupted from the people,
defiant, dangerous, and beguiling,
running towards revolution,
fighting for her realism.

World Wars, Roman slums,
Mussolini, Rossellini,
Luca and little lions,
young lovers and rose tattoos;
life imitated art.

The Eternal City
of cathedral and passion
chants her name like religion.

Mama Roma, earthy goddess
with the violent laugh and epic scream
echoing from the Pantheon.

Magnani is forever:
never betraying her art,
never betraying her people,
forever the She Wolf,
keeping watch over the Open City.

THE MOTHER

Immortal and skin,
arch and ache,
you are the catch-a-fire,
hallelujah, home.

Recite your life,
a maternal masterpiece.
Birth
Burial
Fertility
Forgiveness

If I could rewrite the bible,
write you in Exodus,
religion all the women you are,
all the stories untold.

You, infinite and always,
bone and wine, I and three brothers
carry you forward from earth
and sky.

LESSON PLAN

I went to a fortune-teller on the Upper East Side.

You are meant to have a daughter.

Before I sat down, the weary woman, dressed in gaudy
costume jewelry and moon stones, stared me down
with this revelation, before talk of payment or prayer.

You are meant to have a daughter.
She traces the lines of my hands,
pointing to where the little girl stays tucked
away until she is ready for me to be mother.

Even the woman in my dreams,
the one with the face I can never make out
tells me a daughter is waiting for me.

You are meant to have a daughter.
You are meant to pass on all of your women.
Speak all the women of you loudly—speak them with purpose.

Speak of your great-grandmother, Sara Ross.
Mississippi midwife and farmer
who kept you wrapped in homemade quilts
during summer visits. The one who slept
on your left side.

Retell her thick molasses legs and trifocals,
her wooden porch and presence,
her mason jars of apricots and cha cha—
speak loudly of the catfish lake right by
the house that burned down when she died.

Speak of your grandmother, Mary Ella Starling.
Speak her purple sashes and long fingers,
Speak her cool palms placed on your chest
as she slept on your right side because she
wanted to feel your breathing.

Speak her trips to Paris and St. Lucia, how she
posed in front of the camera, why she stuck her neck out
and kept the right leg slightly in front of the left.
Speak her fragrance. How clean and warm she smelled—
and sometimes like Elizabeth Taylor's Passion perfume.

Speak of the flash of light, the spark in her brain
that took all her memories away. Speak her final days,
when your mother hired the harp player to sit beside
her bed and play to sounds of her heart beating, beating,
gone.

Speak your third cousin, Elsie Smith.
The one you write about all the time.
Speak about her saxophone and pearls,
her sweetheart of rhythm life.

Speak how she played with Lionel Hampton,
Sly & the Family Stone, and for President Eisenhower.
Speak her travels on the USO circuit, her rendition
of "Watermelon Man" that you found, many years later,
its grainy sound spinning over and over on the 45.

Show your daughter the YouTube videos of Elsie,
The all-male jazz caravan, with Hampton and Alan Freed
snapping away, show her the stilettos and the empire waist,
her saxophone making all the screaming teeny boppers
with poodle skirts and pompadours gyrate across color lines.

Finally, speak your mother, Diane Starling Pryor.
Speak her supernatural, her collard greens, her forgiveness,
tell your daughter how she conquered, claimed, and carried on.
Speak her features you back-channel to her.
Speak even though your mother can speak for herself.
It is important that you speak her for the rest of your life.

Speak all these women to the daughter you will have.
She needs to know. She must know the women she will inherit.

What if I have a boy? Then what?

The fortune-teller lifts her head.

The lesson remains the same. Just speak it louder.

NOTES

"Definition": Parnassus definition taken from the Oxford Dictionary and the Collins English Dictionary

Legacy: The original version of this poem was commissioned by Shorefront Legacy

Grateful acknowledgement is made to the editors of the following publications where versions of these poems first appeared:

Poetry Speaks: Who I Am: "Bra Shopping"

A Writers' Congress: Chicago Poets on Barack Obama's Inauguration: "Auto-Correcting History"

America! What's My Name? The "Other" Poets Unfurl the Flag: "Georgia on My Mind"

Ringing Ear: Black Poets Lean South: "Resurrection Under the Moon"

ACKNOWLEDGMENTS

I raise a glass of the finest chianti to the ones who came on my
odyssey and helped this book take first breaths.

A toast to the magnificent chain reaction that is Peg O'Donnell
and Ilyssa Wesche; fairy godmothers of cubicles and Jersey,
who sprinkled pixie dust on me and lead this book to its
Publisher.

Daniel Slager for vision, compassion, and raising the bar on
the publishing experience. Casey O'Neil, Patrick Thomas,
Connor Lane, Casey Patrick, Mary Austin Speaker and the
entire "down for whatever" Milkweed Editions family! Thank
you Mildred Howard for speaking women and borders through
your art and letting it settle on the cover of this book.

Everything starts from the roots: for my Mother and
Stepfather, you given me the space to dream and the speed
to catch them. I owe you everything. My three lighthouse
brothers of heaven and earth, and my Grandparents of
Mississippi Starling/Ross stock, I write your names in the
sky. Love always to the Starling, Fox, and Pryor tribes.

Everything has a middle: Iliana & Aissar El-Khailani, Phoebe
Fox, Ellen Hagan, David Flores, Kelly Norman Ellis, Frank
X Walker, Serena Brommel, Nikky Finney, Mitchell L.H.
Douglas, Ricardo Nazario-Colón, Rachel Eliza Griffiths,
Susan Aurinko, the Affrilachian Poets, Cave Canem,
the Guild Complex, Chicago State University, Spalding

University MFA Program, Northwestern University Press, the support and love mattered.

Everything is everything: Marvin Gaye, Anna Magnani, Bruce Lee, Gwendolyn Brooks, Carolyn Rodgers, Muriel Rukeyser, Elsie Smith "Queen of Sax", fried catfish, salad, key lime pie, fried green tomatoes, juke joints, and every glass of red wine that went into writing this collection.

Cheers!

After studying creative writing at Chicago State University, earning an MFA from Spalding University, and studying publishing at Yale University, PARNESHIA JONES has been honored with the Gwendolyn Brooks Poetry Award, the Margaret Walker Short Story Award, and the Aquarius Press Legacy Award. Her work has also been anthologized in *She Walks in Beauty: A Woman's Journey Through Poems*, edited by Caroline Kennedy and *The Ringing Ear: Black Poets Lean South*, edited by Nikky Finney. A member of the Affrilachian Poets, she serves on the board of Cave Canem and Global Writes. She currently holds positions as Sales and Subsidiary Rights Manager and Poetry Editor at Northwestern University Press. Parneshia Jones lives in Chicago.

Interior design & typesetting
by Mary Austin Speaker

Typeset in Goudy Village

Goudy Village was designed in 1932 by Frederick W. Goudy.
After keeping books for a Chicago realtor for 40 years, Goudy
became one of America's most influential type designers,
designing over 100 typefaces during his lifetime, and authoring
three books on type design. Goudy co-founded the Village Press
in Park Ridge, Illinois in 1903.